IN A MENTAL FOG?

STOP!`
REFOCUS!
FIND YOUR WAY!

BY

MOIRA CARMENATE

Palmetto Publishing Group

Charleston, SC

IN A MENTAL FOG?

Copyright © 2018 by Moira Carmenate

First Edition

Printed in the United States

ISBN-13: 978-1-64111-278-9

ISBN-10: 1-64111-278-6

TABLE OF CONTENTS

CHAPTERS

ABOUT THE AUTHOR

Moira Carmenate is a successful entrepreneur and be-havioural change specialist with nearly forty years' successful track record in business. She has coached, de-veloped and trained business leaders and is still, in her sixties, leading businesses and teams through strategic, cultural and behavioural change.

Moira has overcome many challenges in her life in-cluding being on her own and homeless at seventeen fol-lowing the death of her grandmother. She was raised by her grandparents, the parents of her father, from the age of 15 months when her mother tried to sell her to a strang-er as she didn't want her. Moira's father was in show busi-ness from an early age, a singer in the rock and roll sixties. He left the music business because of corruption within the industry and was not willing to conform to the life-style pressures being suggested to him in order for him to gain success. Being a strong character who was extremely fit, he decided to become an escapologist, carrying out the most challenging and dangerous feats. Some years after the death of his mother and father, he reappeared and briefly came back into Moira's life, even teaching her how to escape from a straight-jacket. He went off on his travels performing as an escapologist and in the late eighties, Moira lost touch with him when he moved to join a circus in Spain. She has just found out that he passed away and is trying to find out what happened.

Moira opened her first business when she was in her twenties with two young children. She built a small hotel business and then five years later sold it to begin a new journey. She loved the business of owning and running a hotel, but she had been living a life constrained by an abusive husband. One day, hoping the sale of the business would complete, she made the decision to leave with only her train fare and her children in a dramatic escape. Her ex-husband threatened to kill her and her children and she had to get them away. An opportunity was offered to her to run a country pub. This provided the first step to her new life and although it wasn't to be her long-term plan, the universe had provided her with the opportunity and an escape route. A few months later she was offered an opportunity to become a Sales Consultant in Financial Services. Within six months she became one of the top producers. She had phenomenal drive and many business opportunities were presented to her. One of those opportunities, which she decided to take, was to open a financial recruitment business in London. Moira would describe herself as being lucky with more lives than ten cats as ironically within a month of joining this business she had a serious car crash and lost her speech and ability to walk. Whilst she was in hospital, the company closed down and she found herself, against Doctor's orders, back on the job market. She was struggling with her speech as a result of a brain injury but had to keep going as she had two young children to feed. With her usual dry sense of humour, she said someone must have felt sorry for her and gave her a job! The job, in a major financial services institution, involved training senior sales consultants in advanced sales techniques using behavioural science. She qualified through an American company and rolled out many workshops on psychology of sales and behavioral change. She was then headhunted into another major financial institution to head up a large sales team of twelve hundred consultants and was the only female Director in the boardroom, not uncommon in those days.

Following the contraction of financial services sector, Moira went on to form her own consultancy and training organization delivering business transformation and cultural change for some of the biggest blue-chip companies in the world.   She is an intrepid entrepreneur and has bought and sold many businesses over the years. Her passion comes from developing people, helping them overcome their fears and helping them build and re-build self-esteem to become the winners they truly deserve to be. She is frequently asked to speak at events and as she speaks from the heart, with a true fighting spirit, she is classed as highly motivational and always an inspiration to male and female audiences alike.

ACKNOWLEDGEMENTS

Thank you to the Universe for giving me all of the life experiences that have enabled me to write this book. Life is a journey and my journey has always been eventful and those events have carved me into the person I am today. Maybe I should apologize!

Thank you to my beautiful family who keep me grounded and provide me with love and support. To my son, Eric, my daughter Chevonne and my beautiful grandchildren who bring sunshine into my life at all times. I am proud of you all and everything you have achieved and are still to achieve. I will be there to support you at every step of your journey and when the day comes that I leave this planet, I will always be there in spirit, the Angel on your shoulder. Hopefully a long way off as I still have chaos to cause.

Thank you to my beautiful husband who has the patience of a Saint. You humour me when I have another brain wave, another business opportunity and now another book (or at least another four currently in my head) which will manifest themselves very soon.

To Michelle who I thank immensely for putting up with me and inspiring me every day to continue on my journey of discovery, you are a very special part of my family and I am grateful you came into my life.

Thank you to my lovely soul sisters, Kathleen, Simran, Sarah, Angela and Gina, who are the best sounding boards, the greatest inspiration and the greatest support. To my other friends along the journey, you all know who you are, thank you for being there.

To all of you, I love you and wish you courage, strength and abundance in your life.

WARNING! THIS BOOK WILL TURN YOUR LIFE INSIDE OUT AND LEAD YOU TO A LIFE OF FREEDOM YOU NEVER THOUGHT POSSIBLE!

Imagine how you will feel when you have full control over your life's events? Imagine being peaceful and not worrying. Imagine not doing things just so you can opt for a quiet life. Imagine you are living life to the full rather than going through the motions. Imagine you can break free from emotional manipulation. Imagine you have abundance and financial freedom and not worrying about how your bills are going to be paid. Imagine you can be the best you possibly can in your working life and in your closest relationships. Imagine you are free to do what you want to do and win. Imagine your dreams will come true.

Now is the time to take control. Don't be afraid to make the changes and live the life you deserve. We will go through a series of steps to help you identify how to live a more enriched life. We will look at why we create our own boundaries and why we don't see our self- imposed blocks and live with them even though they are limiting our own progress. Why we live and work in toxic environ-ments with toxic people without realizing the effect they have on us and our families. Why we live a life that's filled with self-doubt, low self-esteem and stress. Why these stresses and strains create some of the biggest challenges impacting on our health, our love life and relationships, our careers and our finances.

It's time to escape from those restraints, break free and create a positive, enlightened and meaningful life plan. Dream! No-one said you can't dream big. Believe your dreams will come true and put the steps in place to make them happen.

Imagine you are releasing your fears, clearing your mental fog and beginning the life journey you deserve?

Now it's your time – let's begin.

CHAPTER 1

DO YOU KNOW WHO YOU ARE?

I am sure it seems an odd question to ask, do you know who you are? You know your name, your date of birth, father, mother, son, daughter, what you do and where you live so you will be saying, of course I know who I am. You have lived with yourself for many years so who better to know you. The reality is for most of us, we don't really know who we are. It is way too frightening to lift the lid and dive deeply inside to find out who we really are. What if we don't like what we find?

We have been conditioned since we were infants. When we were little, we could play in a carefree way, burst into song whilst dancing wildly and everyone would laugh and think how great it is to be a child. As we got older, we were told, be good, behave, don't run as you might fall and hurt yourself and whilst our parents fulfilled their role as protectors and kept us from harm, sometimes we needed to fall over, feel pain and understand where our risks were. But where did the carefree child go?

The reality is, as you grew up, society influenced you to follow social norms. Be correct, move with caution and against this social norm backdrop, you have developed your own self- preservation system to avoid risk. As you have grown into an adult, that avoidance of risk has enabled you to create your safe haven, an area of comfort where you feel secure and do not face fear.

As you look around at your friends, family, work colleagues you will not see the word fear stamped on their foreheads. Fear is something that is deep within us and we find coping mechanisms to hide it from the outside world. It's firmly rooted in our subconscious mind and it's stopping us from fulfilling our dreams, stopping us from taking even the smallest risk and in turn this is limiting our potential. Fear of saying who you really are in case you face disapproval.

Just like a chameleon, we humans often change our colours to blend into our environment. We don't want to stand out, we don't want to be different, we don't want to be judged. We just want to fit in.

So, let's work out who you are. How are you limiting yourself? How do you know you are not being you? Firstly, not being truly happy within yourself is a clue. When your emotions overtake your reactions to situations, you act against who you really are and try to conform to social norms and pressures.

You need to re-programme your brain and teach yourself how to be yourself in what you say, what you think and what you do whether in relationships, work or at home. But how? Firstly, be aware of your thoughts. Be aware of negative thinking. Look out for it and stop it in its tracks.

Don't let negative thinking cloud your brain. It will take time but once you open your mind and evaluate what you are thinking and why, you can change your mind-set and clear the mental fog. Also identifying your environment is important to keep you on your toes and keep your mind clear as other people's moans and groans will, without you realizing, weigh heavy on you. It is very easy for people to off-load their negativity and often they go off feeling better in themselves, but you are left carrying the weight. Open your antenna and remain tuned in to positivity and block all those negative comments by others. If you imagine a pond filled with beautiful still calm water and then someone throws a big rock into that pond which completely changes the calmness, well that's what happens when you allow that negativity to enter into your positive, still waters. It changes your calm waters into tumultuous stormy waters.

Identify values which are core to you, now and for your future. We all have a built-in set of values against which we aren't willing to compromise. If you are not feeling happy, it may be because you are compromising those values to please other people. Maybe you don't realize what those core values are, but you know when something does not feel right. Our values are own personal code of conduct that guides our behavior. When we consistently follow our personal values, we feel a sense of fulfillment and a feeling of calmness. When we work against those values, like a naughty child, we compromise our beliefs and fall into bad behavior and try and counterbalance, what we deep down know is wrong, to try and make us feel better.

What should a good set of core values look like? We are all individuals, not looking to just fit in to social norms. We have our own individual values, but what are yours? You need to work out what is most important to you, what is your belief system, your own personal code of conduct and what matters. For example, the things that matter most to you may be: family, friends, career, health, holidays, success, sport, finances, music, culture, exercise.

Some people might have the following core values:

A belief that family is of fundamental importance over everything else

A belief that honesty is always the best policy and that trust has to be earned

A belief in maintaining a healthy work/ life balance

A belief in treating others fairly and in a way that you would want to be treated

Some examples of negative values include the following:

> A belief that you are powerless to change your fate or personal situation
>
> A belief that you don't deserve good things
>
> A belief that you don't deserve beautiful relationships
>
> A belief that other people are fundamentally untrustworthy and unloving

Take some time and write down your core values and be true to yourself. This is your work book and your roadmap to happiness. You need to create it with honesty and passion.

If you have never thought about this before maybe take a blank piece of paper and just brain dump and write down the things that come into your head, here are some examples, but remember it's about you – you are not measuring against someone else.

Here are a few descriptive words that can help you.... take ten to twenty minutes and just brain dump your own.

Dependability, reliability, honesty, positivity, passion, respect, perseverance, understanding, tolerance, vision, trust, empathy, steadfast, fidelity, courage, fairness, endurance, patience, spiritual, gratitude, harmony, inspirational, integrity, kindness, loyalty, humility, dignity, credibility, courtesy, conviction, accountability, discipline, ethical, professionalism, responsibility, sincerity, supportive, thankful.

Now let's work some things out. To help you evaluate and create your list of core values, think of some of the best experiences that made you feel fulfilled. What happened and how did you feel? Which of your core values were met?

What was the opposite? When did you face or go through an experience that left you feeling disappointed, sad, confused or even traumatized? What happened and how did you feel? Write down your experience. It may be uncomfortable to dig inside as there will be a lot of emotion surrounding your experience, but sometimes you need to go back before you can go forward. Not to relive, but to gain an understanding and to accept your feelings. Those feelings are not right nor are they wrong, they are your feelings. Which of your core values were not met?

How many situations have you been in that made you feel undervalued, unloved, not worthy? Even though this may hurt, if you truly dig in and write each of those situations, not just one, on a piece of paper or multiple pieces of paper and one by one you will understand why you felt as you did.

Strengthen your core, build your self-awareness and fine tune your own personal antenna and you will take control and stop this happening again. Now all of those pieces of paper, with all those negative events filled with negative emotions, take them one by one and tear them into the smallest pieces and throw them in the fire and let them disappear into smoke. They are now symbolically removed from your life.

To know who you are, you can now identify your core values and what makes you feel good and how your values can be threatened or compromised and make you feel awful. **Write your core values on a card, the size of a credit card and put it in your wallet. Look at this card every morning and remind yourself every day of who you are and truly understand your values**.

Listen to yourself and always remember those values, stand tall and proud, this is part of your journey to freedom and you will radiate confidence when you are being you.

CHAPTER 1

DO YOU KNOW WHO YOU ARE?

1) **How do I limit myself?**
I can't do ----. because! (I will be judged/I may be wrong/Someone will think I am crazy/I might upset someone/I don't want to be seen as different/ I want to fit in)

List the things you do that are limiting you

_____

_____

_____

_____

_____

_____

2) How do I stop limiting myself?
List the things that you will do to stop limiting
yourself

_____

_____

_____

_____

_____

_____

_____

_____

_____

_____

3) **Be aware of getting sucked into negative thinking**

How are other people off loading their negativity on to you in work or at home?

_____

_____

_____

_____

_____

_____

_____

_____

_____

_____

_____

4) **How do I block the negativity and ensure I don't get sucked in?**

_____

_____

_____

_____

_____

_____

_____

_____

_____

_____

_____

_____

5) **What are my core values? – the key things that are important to me**

_____

_____

_____

_____

_____

_____

_____

_____

_____

_____

_____

6) **When did you go against your core values – what happened and what did you feel?**

_____

_____

_____

_____

_____

_____

_____

_____

_____

_____

_____

7) **Which of your core values were compromised?**

_____

_____

_____

_____

_____

_____

_____

_____

_____

_____

_____

_____

8) **How will you protect your core values
and ensure they are not going to be
compromised again?**

_____

_____

_____

_____

_____

_____

_____

_____

_____

_____

_____

CHAPTER 2

DROP YOUR MASK........
BEFORE IT DESTROYS YOU!

Many people live their lives acting and pretending to be something or someone they are not. Wearing a metaphorical mask, acting and telling everyone that everything is fantastic, everything is amazing, they are busy and going in the right direction. All said with conviction, with a big smile, but who is fooling who? Does this sound familiar?

Some people wear that mask for so long that they forget who they truly are and live their lives behind the mask and actually believe what they are telling everyone. Do you recognize that in yourself or others?

How many times have you worn a mask? The reality is, wearing a mask wears you out. It is an exhausting situation to constantly pretend to be someone or something you are not. To be constantly faking it.

You are not a bad person however you have lost your way and got caught up in the masquerade. You have forgotten who you are and what you want from life.

How many times have you, or someone close to you, lost out on something you wanted? Maybe you didn't get the promotion at work, maybe you didn't get to where you wanted to be in a relationship, maybe you lost in a competition, in sport or just didn't get what you wanted. How many times did you then tell everyone, it's ok! I am cool about this! I am not disappointed, I am not fazed by this, I am really ok. Be honest with yourself, the reality was very different and you were completely disappointed, completely gutted and sometimes thrown completely off track as it wasn't what you were expecting. Then we choose our mask, live our life in a masquerade and tell everyone that everything is really wonderful and you have moved on.

Isn't it exhausting wearing that mask? Doesn't it wear you down? In its most destructive form, it can even lead you into a self-destruct mode with extreme and rash behaviors and you go to extreme lengths just to prove a point to the world that you are ok. Don't put yourself at risk, don't lose sight of your core values. You are, underneath everything, not feeling good about yourself. That's ok, it's ok to not be ok as long as you do something about it. So, what do you do? Most people find ways of compensating and trying to make themselves feel better by substituting the feeling of euphoria that the brain creates when we feel good about ourselves. Many people take to bingeing to get that high, whether it be binge drinking, binge sex especially after a relationship breakup, binge shopping, binge eating and even binge working. Anything that will focus your attention away from the problem. These false highs can ironically lead you to the opposite of what you are wanting to create and can lead to depression, anxiety or both.

So how are you going to deal with this? Firstly, you are not alone. Many people feel this way and you know, it's ok to not be ok.

You have blocked your emotions and replaced them with misplaced acceptance. With a rationale and logical reasoning for why you are doing the things you are doing, trying to create alternative highs with all those binge activities and you have ticked the metaphorical "it's ok" box in your head? You need to blow out, you need to shop until you drop, you need to over kill it in the gym, you need to spend every waking hour in the office. It's all logical, right? No, it's wrong! Let's be honest, wearing this mask is killing you, killing your bank balance, taking your mind to places it should not go and putting you on a collision course. What happened to happiness, contentment, satisfaction, gratitude?

So how can you get back on track and put the mask away for good?

Firstly, you need to remind yourself of your values, you know the ones you identified as core values earlier and not the destructive activities you have been following.

Secondly, you need to work out where you want to be. How do you get back on track and how to you get to where you want to be?

You need a plan. You need to detox your life and wash away things and people that are not healthy for you and don't align with your values or with your life plan.

You must get some good habits back into your life and set yourself a structure for your day, your week, your month which will then of course become your year.

If you go to the gym and it has become an obsession rather than part of your healthy living plan, then take a long hard look at what you are doing and why. When you exercise your body, are you looking after your whole body, inside and out. The body is seventy percent water and as you sweat you need to replace that water loss. Take some time to breathe properly before and afterwards. Deep breathing not just shallow breaths. Combine your breathing with your thinking, close your eyes and breathe deep into the depths of your stomach and slowly release. Re-energize your brain with oxygen. Remember as well as all the muscles in your body, the part of you that you should treat like a muscle is your brain. You have been kidding yourself and kidding everyone else, so you need to re-programme your brain, like you do your exercise machines.

Programme your brain to remind you to be grateful. Opening your eyes every morning and looking around you and thanking the Universe for everything you have in your life and everything that is still to come into your life. Cultivating gratitude as the key emotion needs to underpin everything you are doing. Gratitude for the opportunities that have come into your life, good and bad and whether you identified them at the time or not. The Universe is always presenting you with opportunities. You don't always see those opportunities as you are in a mental fog. You may mess up and miss some tremendous opportunities, but that won't stop the Universe putting more in your path. You just need to programme your brain to enable you to open your eyes, believe your self-worth and give you the courage to reach out and take these opportunities with both hands and accept them with gratitude.

You have the power to change what you do, drop your mask, be the real you and identify your life path. However, you need to create daily healthy habits to ensure you get there. Write your journal of where you are going and create your new habits. Start your day with excellence and continue with your plan for excellence until you go to sleep that night.

Be true to yourself and don't live a lie. Showing who you are is a real strength and although you may feel some vulnerability at first, people will respect you for being you.

Have clarity, have purpose and show your soul not your mask.

DROP YOUR MASK-BEFORE IT DESTROYS YOU

1) **List times when you said everything was great when it wasn't**
(you didn't get a promotion/ you split up from a partner / lost in a competition)

_____

_____

_____

_____

_____

_____

_____

_____

2) How did you really feel?

_____

_____

_____

_____

_____

_____

_____

_____

_____

_____

_____

_____

3) **What did you do to compensate and make you feel better?**

_____

_____

_____

_____

_____

_____

_____

_____

_____

_____

_____

_____

4) **In this situation, which of your core values did you compromise?**

_____

_____

_____

_____

_____

_____

_____

_____

_____

_____

_____

_____

5) **How could you have dealt with the situation differently?**

_____

_____

_____

_____

_____

_____

_____

_____

_____

_____

_____

_____

6) **How can you change your thinking to be grateful and believe your self-worth?**

_____

_____

_____

_____

_____

_____

_____

_____

_____

_____

_____

_____

7) How will you ensure your values are not compromised and you will be you?

_____

_____

_____

_____

_____

_____

_____

_____

_____

_____

_____

_____

CHAPTER 3

REMOVE TOXIC PEOPLE & TOXIC SITUATIONS FROM YOUR LIFE

The dictionary definition of toxic is:

poisonous, venomous, virulent, noxious, dangerous, destructive, harmful, unsafe, malignant, injurious, pestilential, pernicious, environmentally unfriendly, mortal, fatal, deadly, lethal.

The question is, why do so many of us put ourselves in toxic environments, toxic relationships and live toxic lifestyles, when the outcome is destructive, harmful, unsafe and potentially deadly?

When it all goes wrong, how many people have asked themselves – why did I not see it at the beginning? These are not stupid people and if you are in a situation like this you should not blame yourself for not seeing, however once you identify what is happening, you should question yourself for not creating a plan and taking positive action to remove yourself or you and your family from such situations.

Living and working in a toxic environment is mentally exhausting when you are constantly walking on eggshells, thinking about every word you say either in frustration or terror.

Let us break it down into environments and relationships to give you an understanding and indicator of what is a toxic environment, what is a toxic relationship and how these situations affect you.

Toxic environments – the workplace

We have all been there! Worked in places full of negativity, full of malicious gossip, full of inadequate people vying for power and trampling on others, lying and doing anything they can in order to be recognized.

Do you remember when you were in school and there were groups of bullies who would shout the loudest and intimidate anyone where they identified the smallest weakness, just to gain power over them?

You would have thought that those toxic behaviours would have been left in the school playground.

How sad it is to realize that those bullies still exist throughout your life and they come in all shapes and sizes and hide behind a variety of masquerades and are especially prevalent in the workplace.

People, often in positions of power, hide behind "it's for the good of the business" as they gather their in-house cavalry to join their battle for power and influence. The ringleader, often when someone has fallen from their position and they think there is a potential opening for them in a higher position, mobilizes his/her troops who will all, in due course, gain something for their loyalty. People who have the need and insecurity to operate in this way are usually covering up their ineptitude and leadership inabilities and brainwashing their followers through manipulation.

You may recall earlier we looked at "do you know who you are?" and how people were like chameleons, changing colours and blending in to their environment, not to be judged or be different, but to fit in. This is exactly what is happening in the workplace. The ringleader, is mobilizing his/her team, ensuring they are blended together and fitting in to what he or she wants them to do.

Sadly, many free thinking and intelligent individuals either do not see what is happening as they trust the ringleader. They do not see his/her game plan, or if they do, they find it easier to go along with this and be part of the group, not wanting to be seen as a disruptor or renegade and be left out in the cold.

With his/her team around him, the ringleader, let's say in this instance, the senior manager or director, finds power with his troops behind him, to be more forthright than he would normally be. Covering inabilities with smokescreens, making himself feel secure and important, they start to create and develop a culture of blame. Why?

It is easy to shout, bully and make people feel inadequate when they cannot deliver either a result or an answer to a question at that moment. This becomes a vicious circle with people almost hiding under their desks when that person comes into the room and certainly ensuring they do not make eye contact as that will be too dangerous and they will be made to look like a fool. We recognize the saying "safety in numbers" however in this situation we have "destruction in numbers".

This "environmental disaster" in the workplace results, at its most disruptive, in teams and individuals failing to deliver results due to lack of trust, fear of conflict, lack of commitment, avoidance of accountabilities and lack of focus on how to deliver results.

So how do we deal with this? Well we can't control the people and challenges that we meet during our life either in relationships or in the workplace, however we can control how we deal with them.

Difficult as it may sound, one key thing to remember, is not to take it personally! You might think that this sounds crazy especially if you feel you are the one in the firing line of the "bully boss". However, it is usually not only one person that feels this way. Often many others will feel the same but are intimidated and don't want to mention it – you are not on your own.

Rise above it – if you don't take it personally, you will see the behavior as childish and remind yourself of bullies in the playground and how you will not be drawn into this manipulative behavior or be part of it.

Use emotional detachment and make sure you remind yourself this is not about you. This is someone who is out of control and often not delivering what the company needs and strikes out as a way of camouflaging the situation. Remember, bullies do want not to see you succeed because they will lose control over you.

However, it is not only bosses who make people's lives hell, it can be anyone in the workplace who contributes to the creation of a hostile environment.

This is usually done by using intimidation, humiliation, and constant criticism to demean you and your work.

Unfortunately, there's much more to workplace bullying than the obvious shouting and screaming. Some passive-aggressive and lesser known bullying examples include purposeful exclusion from meetings/activities, consistently taking credit for your work, sabotaging your work, overloading you with work, purposely withholding information from you and spreading false rumors and gossiping. The list is endless. Often employees will endure bullying from their bosses because they are afraid of losing their job. But letting bullying bosses get away with this unfair treatment can be a bad idea too.

Bullying is bad for your health and unfortunately if you don't confront it, it will continue.

Standing up to your boss is not easy but your health and sanity are at risk so you need to weigh up the consequences and realise that you cannot live and work in this way and why should you? You may risk losing your job but for some confronting a bully and maintaining their sanity and health is their top priority.

If you are going to take the steps to eliminate this behaviour from your life you need to remember a few things. Be assertive, be specific and be confident.

Bullies find it difficult to deal with direct factual confrontation. Do not get emotional and keep things calm and controlled. Place the facts in front of him/her telling them they made a mistake in treating you this way and you are not prepared to allow it to continue.

Give specific examples of times and ways that you have been treated. Be prepared for them to try and shift the blame back to you, remember this is their way of operating, but do not accept this in any way.

At the end of the day, the facts are the facts.

Be confident and professional and rise above their ineptitude.

Continue to work hard and do not spend time discussing this with people you work with. Focus on doing your job professionally and do not let this stear you off track and of course, document everything – you may need it.

By standing up for yourself – you may help other colleagues too.

You just need to remember who you are, what is your life's purpose, keep your focus, be aware and rise above the bullying bad behavior.

Toxic environments – personal relationships

An indicator of toxic relationships at their worst: In Britain 112 women and 22 men are killed every year by their partner or former partner (UK Home Office 2007)

750,000 children a year witness domestic violence (UK Department of Health 2003)

The national society for the protection of children (NSPCC.org.uk) says that 1 in 5 children have been exposed to domestic abuse.

Potentially these figures are much higher as not everyone will answer honestly when polled about their exposure to domestic violence or abuse.

But what is domestic abuse?

The UK government in their Home Office circular 003/2013 (www.gov.uk) extends the definition of domestic violence to include controlling, coercive or threatening behavior as well as violence and encompasses, but not limited to, types of abuse including psychological, physical, sexual, financial and emotional.

Many people say domestic violence was caused by alcohol, insecurity, self-esteem issues, stress or unemployment.

However, one of the real reasons for abuse and violence relates to control. If the "victim" is kept in line and under control, there will be no need to use violence, however the assailant will turn to violence when their controlling tactics fail to work.

There are many examples of toxicity in relationships, from emotional abuse to physical abuse.

Emotional abuse comes in all shapes and sizes when a partner tries to dominate and undermine the other partner, telling him or her they are stupid, too fat or too thin, ugly, can't cook, not good at their job, just some of the many ways to reduce a person's self-confidence. Depending on the situation and whether you have children, they can be used as a pawn with threats to remove the children and turn them against you.

Emotional abuse can be subtle and an example of emotional abuse in action is when a partner cries when you threaten to end what you have realized is an abusive relationship. He or she threatens to kill themselves and says he/she loves you, yet you have been suffering abuse for years.

In its menacing form, abuse exists with a partner who shouts, sulks, smashes things, lies and denies abuse yet threatens to hurt or kill you. Often afterwards they will blame the rage on alcohol, stress or drugs and apologize profusely for their loss of control – until the next time.

There is a danger that in any relationship when these behaviors are sustained over many years they become the norm and ironically you get to a point of acceptance that this is ok. Many people develop coping strategies and find themselves "walking on egg shells" to avoid a trigger point that drives a partner into a rage, i.e. getting to know what actions or words or phrases to avoid. We dare not disagree, keep our opinions to ourselves and keep our heads down. We have been led to believe we are not good enough and are always on diets or always questioning ourselves and not convinced that we can look nice enough or fit enough and be perfect enough for our partners.

Often some of the controlling behaviours stem from jealousy and in its most destructive form will include a partner following you, checking up on you pretending to care. Making it difficult for you to go out and creating obstacles to limit your social activities or relationships with friends and family.

Just like the bully in the playground, or in the workplace, the bully in the personal relationship, taking the male position on this occasion, will flex his muscles, glare, send the children to bed early, giving a warning sign that there could be trouble ahead. In this situation, the bully believes this is normal manly behavior as women are inferior and men are superior.

This bully behavior may be a learned behavior from his own childhood when his mother may have been bullied by his father or he himself may have been bullied at school. This doesn't make it correct or acceptable or that it should become normal behavior. Whatever the form of abuse, it is not acceptable. This behavior often extends to children as well as partners. The abuser exerts strong authoritarian control over the children and often treats them like possessions to support their own emotional failings. This creates a dysfunctional family structure and whilst it may be masked by the cloak of parental guidance it is abusive and sets the wrong behaviours and environment.

You need to protect your children from this type of abuse – it is your duty as a loving parent.

Many people think they cannot live alone and many women believe they cannot cope without a man. This has been reinforced over many years by generations of politicians and media groups, stigmatizing single parents who are usually female. To avoid this stigma of being a single parent, many feel it is easier to stay in the relationship even though it is toxic.

There is actually a warped sense of security in a situation that is known and becomes in some ways "comfortable", even though it is not healthy and very often, not safe. However, it is better in this known situation, than stepping out into the unknown which will create even greater fear than the fear they have become accustomed to.

Find your inner strength and belief in yourself that you are worth so much more.

Now is your time to break free from fear and live the life you deserve.

There are many organisations who provide help and support for people living in abusive situations. If this is you and you feel you are a victim of abuse, please be strong enough to get the help and support you need – NOW.

Toxic People – Pathological liars

What about those people who find their way into your life, relationships, work and you didn't realize they were liars? Why would you? You are a trusting, logical individual.

RULES OF A NARCISSISTIC PATHOLOGICAL LIAR

- Believe your own lies

- Act like you are the victim

- Never admit guilt

- Deny deny deny

- Shift the blame ....then cover up with more lies

It's a sad situation but life is life and when you have been exposed to a pathological liar you should not blame yourself for not seeing it in neon lights.

Why are you the one who is left feeling shattered and thinking "how on earth could I have been involved with this person whether in business or in a relationship"?

Your pain is usually when you ask yourself "why does someone behave like that, especially when I had their best interests at heart"?

Your emotions feel battered, your head is in a state of fog constantly wondering "why" has this person behaved this way. Stop, breathe, it is not you, these are the behaviours of a Narcissist.

The narcissist is highly skilled at telling whatever lies he or she wants, in order to get the upper hand, to win, to create false power, create smear campaigns. They have the capacity to lie and falsify documentation with no fear of redress, as when challenged they will spin whatever fictitious story they can invent to take you off track and leave you scratching your head. They are expert in identifying an ally, the one person who will often, out of innocence, give them an ear and sympathy. Thankfully even the most misguided will eventually start to open their eyes and see that not all is as it seems in the fairy tale world of the narcissistic pathological liar and that they have been duped.

The narcissist is paranoid about being pinned down and attacked and will play the victim until he or she has been vilified. This is especially the case when things are not going the way they should. They will shirk responsibility and accountability at every stage and create smoke screens to cover their ineptitude.

A narcissist is a pathological liar who will lie about anything and everything even when the truth is a better story, as to them it's a means to an end. They have no integrity or conscience and they are not going to change. In fact, because of their egos, arrogance and sense of entitlement, they think they are better than everybody else and see absolutely no reason to change.

The lies are generally nothing to do with you, however, if you are the one who is exposing him or her and about to blow their cover, then the lies will be even more highly charged with emotion and venom.   In this situation, the narcissist will go to extreme lengths to ensure this doesn't happen and if it is happening, they will create a smear campaign to undermine you, their assailant.

So why do narcissists lie?

- For protection – to create a false persona of who they really are

- So that you do not find out about them and their past

- So that they can manipulate and deceive you, for their own gain

- To be in control

- Telling you all that you want to hear

- They don't care about you or your feelings, winning and being in control, is the most important thing

- They get bored very easily

- To gain sympathy they play victim

- They find it easier to lie than to tell the truth

Often the narcissist will display passive-aggressive behaviour patterns. Most frequently these occur in the workplace, where resistance is demonstrated by procrastination, forgetfulness and purposeful inefficiency, especially in reaction to demands by authority figures. This can also occur in personal relationships avoiding direct or clear communication, evading problems, making excuses, blaming others, being obstructive, playing the victim, sarcasm, backhanded compliments, and hiding anger.

It's not your fault

Narcissists are in all walks of life – they can come into your personal life, relationships, work life. You just need to be aware and have your radar tuned to try and avoid, where possible, these devious individuals.

You have been tricked, deceived and manipulated. Somebody was deliberately re-shaping your reality, influencing your decisions and directing your thinking and behavior. In personal and intimate relationships this is intertwined with many mixed emotions, love for the person, fear of breaking away, feeling sorry for them, however generally you are forgetting your own well-being. You are forgetting you.

In your working environment, you often feel sorry for the person however you need to remember that these behaviours are toxic and need to be cut away.

Whatever happened during this time was not your fault.

It is however your responsibility to yourself to let go of any personal feelings you are suffering because you have been duped.

This is their problem, not yours.

To break away from this manipulative situation, you must cut all communication with the individual. No phone calls, no text messages, no e-mails. As long as you continue to engage, **they will continue to try and**

manipulate you. Remember this has become their habit, their domain that they can control and influence. In fact, often they will spend their lives trying to continue to manipulate you! It's not your role to try and get an immature adult to act in a decent, honest and intelligent way.

You need to focus on being you, knowing your truth and living a life being true to yourself and your core values.

Feel relief that you have removed this person from your life. It also is a time to be grateful that you are an honest person and that you have seen such awful behaviour and removed yourself from it.

There is no love lost between you and a narcissistic pathological liar and these actions are not the actions of people with healthy emotions, intelligence and common decency.

The truth always wins.

Let people who do you wrong, leave your life - detox your life! Open your eyes, have clarity and purpose and live the life you deserve.

CHAPTER 3

REMOVE TOXIC PEOPLE & TOXIC SITUATIONS FROM YOUR LIFE

1) **What toxic behaviours have you suffered in personal relationships?**

_____

_____

_____

_____

_____

_____

_____

_____

_____

2)   How did this make you feel?

_____

_____

_____

_____

_____

_____

_____

_____

_____

_____

_____

3) **How has this affected new
    relationships?**

_____

_____

_____

_____

_____

_____

_____

_____

_____

_____

_____

_____

4) How can you ensure you get the best out
    of future relationships and not let the
    past destroy them?

_____

_____

_____

_____

_____

_____

_____

_____

_____

_____

_____

5) What toxic behaviors have you identified in your place of work?
Toxic behaviours by your boss or bosses?

_____

_____

_____

_____

_____

_____

_____

_____

_____

_____

_____

_____

6) **How has this affected you & how did it make you feel?**

_____

_____

_____

_____

_____

_____

_____

_____

_____

_____

_____

_____

7) **Reminding yourself of your core values, how would you now handle this differently?**

_____

_____

_____

_____

_____

_____

_____

_____

_____

_____

_____

8) **What Toxic behavior have you identified by colleagues?**

_____

_____

_____

_____

_____

_____

_____

_____

_____

_____

_____

_____

9) How did this affect you and how did it make you feel?

_____

_____

_____

_____

_____

_____

_____

_____

_____

_____

_____

_____

10) Reminding yourself of your core values how would you now handle this differently?

_____

_____

_____

_____

_____

_____

_____

_____

_____

_____

_____

_____

11) Who have you worked with or had a
relationship with only to find they are a
liar?

_____

_____

_____

_____

_____

_____

_____

_____

_____

_____

12) How did you find them out?

_____

_____

_____

_____

_____

_____

_____

_____

_____

_____

_____

13) **What are you doing to cut this out of your life?**

_____

_____

_____

_____

_____

_____

_____

_____

_____

_____

_____

_____

CHAPTER 4

FIND THE HAPPINESS YOU DESERVE

If you were on your death bed, would you be thinking, I wish I had followed my dream and had the courage to do what I always wanted to do? At that point, who is going to challenge you and say your dream was crazy? No-one! and at that point, of course, it is also too late. Why would you allow this to happen?

Imagine how you would feel if happiness and fulfillment were within your reach? Unfortunately, we are the ones who put blocks in the way and we don't always realize we are doing it. In reality, very little is needed to have a happy life as it is all within yourself, within your thoughts, within your mind and within your control.

I often recall being asked "are you happy?" and responding, "well that depends, can you define happiness"? Thankfully, I grew up, realized the things that are important to me, what true happiness is to me and what I am grateful for.

Happiness will be something different to all of us. There isn't a right or wrong version. I love this quote from Oscar Wilde "be yourself, everyone else is already taken".

Some people you see may appear to constantly give off a happiness vibe and you may wonder what do they have that makes them this way? What are they are doing, that makes them happy all of the time? You may think, I wish I could be like them. However, you do have the power to change your thinking and find your happiness, it's in your own hands right now.

Firstly, start by appreciating what you have. You are alive, so you have breath. Wherever you are at this moment, step outside and look around you. What do you see? The sky, the trees, the buildings, the architecture, can you feel the breeze on your face, can you hear the birds? Even in the most built up areas of a city centre, there are birds. Have you ever stopped and listened to the birds singing? Have you ever stopped and said "thank you" to your God or the Universe for everything you have? Do it now, but really mean it and smile, breathe, appreciate and demonstrate your gratitude.

Every morning, if you just take a minute to look around you, be grateful and say thank you for what you have before you set about your tasks for the day. Then as you recognize the little things in life and that you truly have something to be grateful for, you will start to feel the happiness that may have been hiding within you.

Too many people live their lives thinking, I will be happy if I have a new car, I will be happy if I have a big house, I will be happy if I have lots of money, I will be happy if I win the lottery. These are material things and if you think, not too hard, how many people you know who have many of those things and are not happy. They still have tortured lives, not content with something, whether it be their looks, their family situation or their relationships. In fact, it is only when you realize that happiness is not associated with material things and when you let go of the search for those things, you will find there is a deeper joy and satisfaction within you.

It is similar in relationships. How many times have you thought if only I had a partner or if only I had the right partner? Whilst it is nice to share your life with someone, firstly you have to be happy in your own space. Be at one with yourself, know yourself, love yourself and take care of yourself. How can you let someone into your life when you are not truly at one with yourself? That person is not going to fill the void.

If you feel deep sadness, maybe after the loss of a partner or the end of a relationship, it is possible to feel happy again. You can heal your soul.

Firstly, you have to identify the things that could be limiting your happiness.

You may be hanging on to situations that have happened in the past. We can be our own worst enemy, focusing on what we can't do rather than what we can do. With mental blocks built from past failures, either in relation-ships, in work or in business, we create a block of fear that limits us from moving forward. We whisper things to our-selves that we wouldn't dream of saying to a friend. If a friend had some trauma, a broken relationship or lost their job, we would be trying to help them get back on track, feel good about what they have achieved rather than what they have lost. However, when it comes to ourselves, we have a real knack of metaphorically beating ourselves up with blame and doubt. You can't change things that are in the past, but you can learn from them and by being aware you can turn the negatives into positives.

The good news is, you have the power to change your outlook. You have the power to be who you want to be and to be awesome. Why would you be anything less?

Firstly, you have to believe in yourself. You attract what you give off – so be aware what you are thinking and how you are every day. Imagine your head is a glass bowl and everyone can see inside and see what you are think-ing! I am sure if you carry this visual in your head, you will be more conscious of your thoughts and how they could be viewed. Better to be viewed as someone who is inspira-tional because of your inner beliefs and selfless thoughts for others. Believe in you and how you can share positivity with others.

Create daily positive habits. It takes sixty-six days for the brain to convert a daily habit into an automatic routine.

Your mental health and well-being is determined by how well your brain can perform mental processes like remembering things and learning things. A healthy brain is just as important as a healthy body. Many of the things you do to keep your body healthy can also keep your brain healthy.

Physical activity increases blood flow to the brain. If you don't already have an exercise plan, try to include 30 minutes of physical activity into your schedule every day. Choose something you enjoy doing, like walking, swimming, dancing.

Be aware of what you are consuming. The food and drink you put into your body is important to your physical and mental well-being and for your overall health. Make a conscious effort to add five healthy foods to your daily diet and improve your lifespan.

Feed your body with nourishment, feed your brain with positivity and exercise daily.

Once you have this vitality you will shine and radiate confidence. When you shine with this new-found confidence, smile more, be brighter, be you, others will shine with you. It's contagious.

Your happiness contributes to the happiness of the world – smile and others smile back. Don't put on hold waiting for the perfect situation or perfect moment. Live in the now, avoid mental fog and enjoy everything you have and everything you are. You are your own unique being.

FIND THE HAPPINESS YOU DESERVE

1) What has made you unhappy?
In relationships

_____

_____

_____

_____

_____

_____

_____

_____

_____

_____

_____

_____

In work/business

_____

_____

_____

_____

_____

_____

_____

_____

2)   **What are you doing just to fit in rather than being you?**

_____

_____

_____

_____

_____

_____

_____

_____

_____

_____

_____

_____

3) How will you control your thoughts and emotions to ensure those things that made you unhappy, won't happen again?

_____

_____

_____

_____

_____

_____

_____

_____

_____

_____

_____

4) **List at least 10 things – no matter how small – that have made you happy?**

1. _____

2. _____

3. _____

4. _____

5. _____

6. _____

7. _____

8. _____

9. _____

10. _____

_____

_____

_____

5) **If anything was possible, what would you want to do that would make you the happiest person in the world?**

_____

_____

_____

_____

_____

_____

_____

_____

_____

_____

_____

6) **How will you describe the happiness you feel at that moment?**

_____

_____

_____

_____

_____

_____

_____

_____

_____

_____

_____

7)   You need to remind yourself to look
     after yourself. What new habits will you
     create to nourish your brain and your
     spirit?

_____

_____

_____

_____

_____

_____

_____

_____

_____

_____

8) **What exercise will you include in your daily routine?**

_____

_____

_____

_____

_____

_____

_____

_____

_____

_____

_____

_____

9) **What will you add to your diet to ensure you are nourishing your mind and body?**

_____

_____

_____

_____

_____

_____

_____

_____

_____

_____

_____

CHAPTER 5

DREAMS DO COME TRUE

It's important for you to have dreams and aspirations. Otherwise what are you striving for and where are you going? Walt Disney said, "All our dreams can come true if we have the courage to pursue them."

Imagine your dreams can come true? How are you going to feel? Do you remember how to dream? Yes, sometimes we are so caught up in all the mental fog in our head, we forget it is possible to dream. How might you feel if you let go and let your imagination run free?

Let me tell you a story about Sanjo who was born into a circus family. His mum and dad were trapeze artists in a travelling circus, in fact his whole family lived and worked in the circus. His great grandfather had been a lion tamer, his grandfather was an escapologist and his grandmother his glamorous assistant. Life for Sanjo, was filled with variety, changing scenery, changing towns, changing friends, a life always on the move. To the outside world this was a life full of glamour, mystery, fun and adventure – every child's dream. Mum wore the most glamourous sequined costumes and performed the most daring double trapeze swings with dad. Every night they would perform nightly on the high wire, almost defying physics by flying effortlessly above the crowds. Crowds sat below them and around the circus ring, waiting to be thrilled and never realizing that in every show the flying trapeze artists risked their lives should something go wrong.

Circus life was a very hard life filled with long working days and nights and constantly packing up and moving from town to town and country to country. In between the moves, the performers constantly practiced ensuring their acts appeared flawless to the audiences.

From a very young age Sanjo had to help with the daily chores that came with circus life. First thing in the morning, he had to help his mother clean their mobile caravan. Sanjo's family had a beautiful caravan, one of the largest within the travelling circus troupe. They had saved their money over the years and the caravan homes passed through the generations. Over the years they changed from a simple caravan and trailer until they upgraded to a caravan with an interior that resembled something similar to a glitzy Mayfair apartment, with beautiful ivory and black luxurious drapes, stunning ivory sofas, gold chande-liers and beautiful shiny cherry wood floors. Sanjo's Mum was very proud of their home and intent on ensuring that everyday Sanjo helped her keep this glitzy caravan looking it's best as it was the family's pride and joy and to the fam-ily it represented a token of their hard work.

When Sanjo had finished helping Mum clean their caravan he, along with the other circus kids, would have to help with chores in the big top.

When they arrived in a new town, the riggers would all get together to erect the big top. The first sign to let people know the circus had arrived in town, was the pres-ence of the tall red and white stripy canvas with billowing flags blowing in the wind. The roof of the big top could be seen from far and wide and then it was the job of the men of the circus to rig the seating around the three rings that would become the performance areas for all the fabulous circus acts.

Sanjo enjoyed going out with the team to put posters into shops, bars, libraries, schools and as many places as they could to promote the circus. He loved to see the new towns, new places and new faces. He found it really ex-citing wondering of all the people they would meet, who would come to see the circus when it opened. Life as a circus child was disciplined and although it looked ad-venturous and fun to those outside of circus life, Sanjo actually longed for stability. He wanted to have friends that he could share stories with, could play with and go to their homes and sleep over like normal kids. He wanted to belong.

Many nights, sitting outside their caravan, after the circus performances had finished, Sanjo would recall long conversations with his grandfather who died ten years ago. His grandfather also grew up within the circus and became the principal lion tamer. His grandfather's circus days were very different as there were a lot more riskier acts with wild animals than those allowed today. He remembered as a little boy, watching his grandfather go into the ring in his long black coat, trimmed with red and gold braid. They would release the lion into the fenced cage within the ring and his grandfather would stand firm and stare at the lion as the lion roared loudly. The crowds would gasp as his grandfather got closer to the lion and then when he was right in front of the lion's face, he would get the lion to calmly sit down.

Sanjo asked his grandfather how he had the courage to face the lion and his grandfather told him he didn't have any fear of the lion as the lion was his friend and they trusted each other. The lion knew that he wasn't in danger and between them they developed a mutual respect and deep trust. Sanjo wished he had the courage to face the lion, like his grandfather, but he feared the lion's roar, in fact deep down Sanjo feared many things but covered up his fear by joking and doing silly things.

As the years went on, Sanjo took on many roles in the circus, but above all he loved being the clown. He loved to make people laugh and that became his passion. He wanted to make people happy. He would spend a long time painting his face with the special white liquid, paint his wide eyes with pale blue powder, put on his big shaggy red and yellow wig and finally put on the big red nose that everyone expected a clown to have. He had various costumes but he particularly liked the billowing red silk pants, bright yellow silk shirt, black and red braces and his big black shiny shoes that were enormous and looked like they were far too big for him. He wanted to make sure his clown face and costume was a bright and funny one so that he would always make people laugh. Creating happiness in others was so important to Sanjo, he believed that no matter what was going on in someone's life, if they could laugh, they could set themselves free from any pain they were feeling.

However, if Sanjo was honest with himself, there was something missing in his own life. Beneath the white painted face and behind his jovial activities to make others laugh, when he was on his own in the quiet of the night, he felt an emptiness and he knew deep down in his soul, something was missing but he didn't know what.

One night after the performances had finished, he sat outside the family caravan, counting the stars as he often did and wondered where his life would go. What was his true purpose in life? He looked up at the dark night sky with the bright twinkling stars and thought how beautiful the night sky was and who else could be looking at those bright twinkling stars in another land. Were they looking at the same stars? He remembered many times when he was a little boy, counting stars with his beloved grandfather and that night as he counted the stars, he recalled a story that his grandfather told him

His grandfather told him about a clown called Barnaby who grew up in the circus a hundred years ago. Barnaby would talk about a secret treasure chest that was buried in a far- away land. The chest, as far as the story was told, held precious treasure and the finder would gain the power to change the world. The location of this treasure chest was on a map that one of the older clowns found many years before. They spoke about an old key that was hidden in a book and that key would open the secret treasure chest. Barnaby was so sad that no-one believed his story and he often cried when he told it. He was a clown, why would someone believe him. He was a joker and only there to make people laugh. No-one ever took clowns seriously, but Barnaby's story passed through the generations. However, Sanjo's grandfather wondered whether there could be some truth in this story and Sanjo often thought how powerful he could become if he found this secret chest.

Sanjo went to bed recalling the lovely stories from his grandfather. He fell asleep quickly and drifted into a dream filled slumber. In his dream he is walking along a winding stone path and follows the path down to a winding river. It is a warm sunny day and the sky above is bright blue and not a single cloud in the sky. He feels the warm sun on his head and feels the heat from the sun warming his whole body. At the side of the path, the grass seems even greener than normal as the sun shines brightly. He walks peacefully towards the river, enjoying the contentment, listening to the birds singing in the trees. He moves off the path and walks on the soft green grass and he feels like he is walking on air. As he continues towards the river, he sees someone in a small boat, he is fishing and whistling a tune. Sanjo smiles to himself and thinks how relaxed the man looks in his tranquil domain quietly waiting for a fish to take the bait. Sanjo continues to walk alongside the river, feeling blessed in the tranquility. He listens to the rustle of the trees as a gentle breeze dances through the leaves. As he continues along the riverside, ripples of water stroke the small rocks, creating a soothing sound. He walks along a path through corridors of tall pine trees that line the side of the river and his senses are awakened by the clean smell of fresh pine. He breathes deeply enjoy-ing every moment and continues his stroll until he comes to a meadow. How calm he feels as he looks at the expanse of green land in front of him.

Sanjo spots something odd and can't quite make out what it is. As he slowly gets closer, he realizes it is some-one sitting on a bench. Someone in a dark grey robe with a draped hood softly covering their head and framing a deeply lined sallow skinned face. It is an old man and although Sanjo is at first reluctant to continue, however the old man raises his head and gently smiles and beckons Sanjo to come and sit with him on the bench. Hesitantly, Sanjo moves closer to the bench and sits beside the old man. He somehow feels like he is intruding in the old man's space.

After a couple of minutes as Sanjo sits on the bench he feels strangely at peace beside the old man, who reaches out a soft, deep lined hand to Sanjo. The old man raises his head and says to Sanjo "thank you for coming to me, I have been waiting a long time for you". "I want to share a story with you". Sanjo is surprised, why has he been waiting for me? The old man continues, he tells Sanjo that when he was a young man, he wanted more and more freedom to choose his life's path however he had to work to help his family and felt obliged to stay within the boundaries of his family's business as that was what was expected of him. He felt he had a duty to stay although he longed for more from his life. This often led to arguments within his family however the old man explained that because it was expected of him, he felt he had an obligation to stay. The one thing that the obligations could not prevent, was the old man's dreams. He had a recurring dream that he would travel to a far-away land to find hidden treasure and every time he dreamt the same dream it became more and more vivid. The old man described how he knew, to the very spot, where this treasure was buried but didn't know how he could leave the family to go and find it. He had worked hard within his family's business and felt he had fulfilled his obligations as a son.

One day after waking from his dream, he decided it was his time to take action. He told Sanjo that he had a little money saved and he approached his family and explained about his dream and how he felt he must go and find his purpose. To his surprise, his family were very supportive and felt sad that he had been unable to share his desires with him. However, he had now told them and they gave him their blessing and he felt a new energy and excitement that he could follow his dream. He had packed a couple of things in a little bag and headed off on his journey to find his treasure. He knew that he would have to find work along the way to fund his trip and he was confident that he would find something. His journey took him to many towns and often he would look for work helping in the fields or helping in a hostelry. It was a journey filled with many challenges. One time he asked if he could help in a hostelry in exchange for food and a bed for a couple of nights. The landlord agreed to let him work and stay for a couple of nights however on the last day as he woke up and got ready to leave, he discovered that someone had stolen all his money. He was distraught and angry, but he could not accuse the landlord as he had helped him in the first place. What was he going to do? Had the landlord tricked him or was it one of the other people who stayed in the Inn? He had no money, but he needed to continue on his journey. He had to find free transport to the next town and luckily someone was heading in the same direction and kindly allowed him to travel with him. What was he going to do for food and drink when he got there? He stopped at another hostelry and again asked the Landlord if he had work for him however the Landlord did not need any more staff. He asked the Landlord if there was some other work he could do in exchange for food and a place to sleep and eat. The Landlord found some work for him to build a pen for the pigs and he happily undertook the work. The Landlord had recognized how diligently he had worked and paid him some money each day as he felt that just by giving him food and a place to sleep was less than his worth.

Whilst he was there working, the landlord's daughter, Maria, would bring him drinks and food. He noticed how beautiful she was with the darkest dancing eyes he had ever seen. Every day he would hope she would come again so he could see her. When he looked in her eyes, all the tension that he felt melted away. He had never experienced something like this before. One day when he had worked many hours, she brought him some food and sat talking with him. He told her about his dream and that he was on a journey to find treasure. She was fascinated by his story and agreed that everyone should have a dream and be true to themselves to follow that dream. With every hour that passed in the day, he waited for the moment she would come to see him. One day he said to her that he wanted to stay and spend his life with her. She was touched by his words and felt the same however, she told him he still needed to follow his dream, or he would live with regret. Some weeks passed and with some sadness, he continued his journey with Maria's words firmly in his heart. Maria was correct, if he didn't follow his dream he would live with regret.

Eventually after many more months of travelling from town to town, he arrived at the location where he believed the treasure was buried. He couldn't see anything and found a spade to dig the ground at the place he thought it should be. He dug and dug, deeper and deeper, but nothing was there. He sat on a stone, despondent with his head in his hands, feeling a sense of despair and disillusionment. Had he come all this way, suffered hardship, been robbed of his possessions, worked in fields, hostelries and building in vain. He had worked really hard but more than anything, he had left behind the woman he loved, all for nothing?

What had been the purpose of his journey?

He looked at the sky above and by this time night had fallen and the sky was dark. There was one bright shining star beaming down on him. As he looked at the shining star, he thought about Maria and although she was far-away he wondered if she was looking at the same star. Then he realized, his journey was about awakening the love that had been buried in his heart. No gold or diamonds could replace the treasure that he had in his heart for Maria. He realized, after all of these years, that the treasure was within him. Finding peace within himself and knowing his life's purpose was worth all the material things that money or gold could buy. He could not believe how he felt inside, how strong and how energized. This was something he had never felt before. He stood up, looked up to the bright shining star and in his mind, he saw Maria's beautiful face and dark dancing eyes and shouted loudly "thank you Universe". It has taken me many hard years and many hard knocks to realize who I am and to have deep gratitude for what I have in my life. He breathed deeply and felt profound peace and happiness.

As he walked away a storm suddenly began and the wind blew stronger and stronger. He hadn't seen winds like this before, it was terrifying. He wrapped his arms around a tree and tried to hold tightly to avoid being blown away. The wind continued, it whistled loudly and created a tornado like vortex. Universe – what is happening? The howling wind circled the stone he had been sitting on until it blew the stone yards away from its spot.

As quickly as the storm began, it stopped! Shocked at what was happening he regained his balance and walked to where the stone had been. Etched into the earth was the sign of a star. What on earth was this? Quickly, he got a stick and dug and dug below the surface until in amazement – there it was – the treasure chest he dreamt about. It was a small wooden chest. He opened it, but it was full of stones. How could this be? Was his dream a lie? Treasure? There are only stones here! In anger he grabbed each stone and threw each one as far as he could. Until, when the stones had been all thrown away, he saw what looked like an old piece of paper. What was this? Reaching into the chest, he gently removed the paper. It was an old parchment scroll. Delicately he unrolled the scroll worried that he would damage it. What was written on this scroll?

Your guide to an abundant life
(he who follows this guide shall live an enlightened,
abundant life with the power to inspire others and change
the world)

- Your life is a gift, use it wisely and start every day with gratitude, say "Thank you Universe".

- Your happiness contributes to the happiness of the world, smile and others will smile too.

- Respect others' opinions, but don't let others define you, you are your own person.

- Don't hold anger or resentment, it is like holding a snake – you will be the one who gets poisoned.

- Don't be afraid to fail as failure takes you on an enlightened path to winning.

- Don't put happiness on hold. Don't live in your head, worrying and waiting for the right things to come into your life – live in the now and enjoy.

- Always achieve your fullest potential in everything – don't limit yourself – like a butterfly evolving from a caterpillar, you must find your wings and fly.

- Have courage – believe in yourself – if you don't believe in you, how can you expect others to believe in you?

- Awaken your senses. The Universe is always throwing you opportunities, but you don't always see them as your antenna is closed off to the signals. Wake up - the Universe is guiding you.

- Find your true purpose – you owe it to yourself and to the Universe.

- Persevere – when things get tough, remember your journey, pick yourself up and go forward, you owe it to yourself to be grateful and learn from the experience.

- Love yourself, for without love for yourself you limit your capability to love others.

These are your rules of life.
It is your duty to the Universe to live by these rules, shine brightly and help others find their light.

He put the scroll back into the old chest and covered it with the old blanket that Maria had given him. He put it in his bag and started back on his return journey to Maria. He realized that no gold or gems in the world could replace the treasure he had in his heart for Maria and reading the scroll highlighted how he should live his life. The Universe had sent him many signals throughout his life, but his brain was often in fog and without realizing he constantly blocked the signs. He had to experience some hard knocks before he realized what he actually had in his own hands.

Sanjo had listened in amazement and thanked the old man for sharing his amazing story and the importance of having a dream but also having a clear purpose and having love in your life.

He got up and with immense gratitude kissed the deep lined hand of the old man and headed back along the riverbank to where he started his walk. As he walked, feeling grateful for the experience, he looked back at the meadow and the old man had gone.

After what seemed like many hours, Sanjo woke up but felt slightly bewildered. He felt that he had received a message from his grandfather about the treasure chest in a far-away land. Could this be true? Could this be real? Should he ignore it?

Why would he dream this now? Why would the dream be so vivid?

Why did he meet the old man on the bench?

The next day Sanjo went about his daily chores, got his costumes ready for his evening performance but kept replaying the dream in his head.

He kept telling himself that this was just a dream and dreams are fiction in your head. Sanjo continued through the day and performed in the evening as normal, making everyone laugh at his antics. When he finished, he cleaned off his make-up and sat outside the caravan looking up to the night sky – looking desperately for some sign but no sign came. Frustrated, he went to bed. When he woke up in the morning, he felt he must go to the caravan that had the old archives and old costumes from the circus troupes from years ago. Something was pulling him there.

It was custom within the circus world to keep the old costumes and props as part of the circus heritage. What may he find in the old packing cases? He had a feeling that there was something there for him, something that would drive him to check through the mountain of dusty packing cases. One by one he opened the old chests with trapeze artist costumes, ring master top hats and tails and many old props from years of circus entertainment. Eventually, Sanjo opened a chest that had old clown costumes, wigs, props and old-style clown make up. Sanjo wondered how many stories could be told from all the years' props in these packing cases. Remembering his grandfather's story about the old clown Barnaby, he wondered if some of these props were his. He picked up an old yellow silk shirt, similar to Sanjo's own favourite yellow silk shirt and he smiled to himself as it had a big letter B embroidered on it...B for Barnaby. How odd that Sanjo's favorite shirt was almost identical to this old yellow silk shirt that belonged to Barnaby the clown. As he held the old shirt up, he noticed something, a paper, in the breast pocket. Delicately he tried to remove the paper, conscious of the fact it was very old and could fall apart. What was it? As he opened the paper, his heart started to beat faster as he realized it was a map. Was this the map in his dream? The map his grandfather spoke about? The map giving the location of the precious treasure chest? It was here all the time, within the old props caravan, but the story mentioned a book with a key, where was the key? Like a man possessed, Sanjo moved all the old chests, opening them one by one until he came to the bottom, the very last one. He opened it and inside was another smaller chest with a book sitting on top of it. He picked up the old book, opened the cover, turned the first page and he found a secret compartment that revealed an iron key. This was it, the key to the treasure chest that the old clown Barnaby had mentioned but no-one took him seriously. But was this the chest right here? Had Barnaby actually found the chest? Sanjo took the key from the old book and tried to open the chest. It was a bit sticky but after a few tries it opened. He opened it and there inside was an old parchment scroll. He delicately opened the scroll and read it. **Your guide to an abundant life (he who follows this guide shall live an enlightened, abundant life with the power to inspire**

others and change the world). One by one he read it all, the rules of life, a truly inspirational way to live your life.

Sitting on the chest for what seemed like hours, Sanjo thought deeply and remembered his dream and the old man on the bench. He remembered what the old man had said about finding the scroll and the rules of life which, if he followed, would give him more treasure than he could ever dream of. He thought about Barnaby, the old clown as he was holding the key. Maybe Barnaby had been unable to read, which would have been quite normal at that time, and he would not have realized the significance of the scroll. As Sanjo pondered deeply he felt to him the key represented a symbol of life, of opening and closing. Opening his mind, his heart, his thoughts to where he was going in life and what he truly desired and closing the door on things and people that limited him from achieving those desires. This would lead him to a truly abundant life.

Now it was his time to carve his future and he needed to have a clear plan of where he was going, what he wanted and how he would get there. Nothing could stop him as he would be driven by his passion as well as the experiences, he had been fortunate to gain throughout his life.

He recalled the old man on the bench and his words that the most valuable treasure was the treasure within his heart, knowing his life's purpose, sharing it with love and being grateful for everything he had experienced in life.

Over the coming months, Sanjo created his plan. Like the old man on the bench who told the story about working in his family's business and feeling obligated to stay for fear of letting them down and then when he shared with them his desire to follow his dream, they were so support-ive, now this was Sanjo's time. He, like generations before him, had grown up and worked within the travelling circus and he felt that this was what was expected of him.

Sanjo decided, as his passion was still to make people laugh and make people happy, he now needed to channel this in a different way to fulfil his life's purpose. He need-ed to share with his family that he wanted to follow his dream and not stay within the constraints of the travel-ling circus although he had appreciated his life and every-thing the family had done for him. This was now his time.

Sanjo decided to open a school for Clowns. He wanted to help other people achieve their dreams. He relayed to others the story about the treasure chest, the scroll and the written rules of life. This was his time to help other people fulfil their dreams and by doing so he would fulfil his.

Sanjo's clown school grew and grew and became the most highly acclaimed clown school in the world. To give something back to humanity, Sanjo, with the help of his international clowns, used laughter to help break down barriers in mental health, helped in hospitals, schools and took laughter workshops into worldwide businesses.

Sanjo had truly found his life's purpose and was now, following the Guide to an Abundant life, helping others find their true purpose.

Now it is your time to dream. Everything is possible and there are no limits – only the limits you put on yourself. Imagine, dream big and feel the joy.

DREAMS DO COME TRUE

1) **You only have one life, this is it – what is your dream?**

_____

_____

_____

_____

_____

_____

_____

_____

_____

2) Where are you now in your life?

_____

_____

_____

_____

_____

_____

_____

_____

_____

_____

_____

_____

Job?

_____

_____

_____

_____

_____

_____

_____

Relationships?

_____

_____

_____

_____

_____

3) **If you could wave a magic wand, what would you change?**

_____

_____

_____

_____

_____

_____

_____

_____

_____

_____

_____

_____

4) **Now picture in your mind what your new life would look like?**

Take a moment, close your eyes, visualize where you are, who you are with, what you are wearing, what is the environment around you...now write the detail

_____

_____

_____

_____

_____

_____

_____

_____

_____

_____

5) You have visualized what your new life looks like, now how are you feeling in this new life? Close your eyes and feel the moment...now write down how you are feeling in this new life?

_____

_____

_____

_____

_____

_____

_____

_____

_____

6) **What are the main differences between your life now and the picture you just created in your mind?**

_____

_____

_____

_____

_____

_____

_____

_____

_____

_____

7) **What will this new life bring to you or you and your family when you achieve it?**

8) **What will you do more of and less of to bring your dream to life?**

   More of:

   _____

   _____

   _____

   _____

   _____

   _____

   _____

   _____

   _____

   _____

   _____

Less of:

_____

_____

_____

_____

_____

_____

_____

_____

_____

_____

_____

_____

Now let´s get a plan in place and you can

begin living your dream.....

CHAPTER 6

CREATE YOUR PLAN & START LIVING YOUR DREAM

When your current life is far removed from the life you want, what are you going to do about it?

Sometimes we are forced to stop and take a long hard look at where we have been, where we are and where we should be going. Often the Universe throws us a storm, stirs things up and throws us into a corner where we have no choice but to take stock and take action. The shock tactics of the Universe.

The reality is, many of us, end up drifting through life in a mental fog. We get tired, caught up running like a hamster on a wheel and can´t actually see where we are going. We get disorientated and lose our focus. This leads to frustration which can cause us emotional stress and brain fatigue and we give up.

To achieve your own personal success, for you, for your family, you need to take control of your life. Success doesn´t happen by accident.

You need to know where you are going, when you want to get there, how you will get there and really importantly, keep on track and remind yourself why you want to get there. Without a passion, perseverance and desire to do something, you will fall by the wayside and go straight back to meandering in your mental fog.

Now, stop your procrastination and avoidance let's get your plan underway.

Firstly, find your clarity and clear the fog. Be specific and clear on what you want – what are your goals? Write them down, take time and visualize yourself achieving them and how you feel. There is no limit, they are your goals and it's your time to go and achieve them. The old Acronym for goal setting is goals need to be SMART. – Specific, Measurable, Achievable, Realistic and Timebound.

Goals need to be specific – you need to know what it is you are wanting to achieve. Goals need to be measurable – you need to know how you will know that you are on track. Goals need to be achievable – you need to set something that you can actually get to. It's ok to set another set of goals once you achieve the first. Follow your ambitions in stages and you will find such a sense of accomplishment that will drive you on to the next goal.

Goals need to be realistic – it's ok to dream big, but no point of thinking you are going to discover and fly to a new planet. Goals need to be timebound – you need to set some timelines around when you are going to achieve your goal or you will just drift.

GOAL 1:

- What am I going to achieve?

- What date will I achieve it by?

- How will I achieve it? (what do I need to do on a daily basis to get to my goal?)

- How will I check if I am on track?

- What will I reward myself with when I achieve my goal?

GOAL 2:

- What am I going to achieve?

- What date will I achieve it by?

- How will I achieve it? (what do I need to do on a daily basis to get to my goal?)

- How will I check if I am on track?

- What will I reward myself with when I achieve my goal?

GOAL 3:

- What am I going to achieve?

- What date will I achieve it by?

- How will I achieve it? (what do I need to do on a daily basis to get to my goal?)

- How will I check if I am on track?

- What will I reward myself with when I achieve my goal?

GOAL 4:

- What am I going to achieve?

- What date will I achieve it by?

- How will I achieve it? (what do I need to do on a daily basis to get to my goal?)

- How will I check if I am on track?

- What will I reward myself with when I achieve my goal?

GOAL 5:

- What am I going to achieve?

- What date will I achieve it by?

- How will I achieve it? (what do I need to do on a daily basis to get to my goal?)

- How will I check if I am on track?

- What will I reward myself with when I achieve my goal?

You can have as many goals as you wish, just remember, to be serious about achieving them you need to factor them into your daily habits and create a workable plan to ensure you are going in the right direction and stay on track.

Don't be afraid to reach out to friends and family. Voice your passion for your new life and new you, achieving your goals and your life's dream. You will be amazed how many people will do everything they can to help you.

Be honest with yourself, share with others and you will live an inspired life and as you shine with your new found super confidence you will most certainly inspire others along the way.

CHAPTER 7

TAKE CONROL OF YOUR LIFE –
GET OUT OF THE FOG

How will you feel when you are controlling your life and have a clear vision of where you are going? This is your life, nobody else's life. You need to be in the driving seat and you need to have a clear vision of where you are going and not go along with things just because you want to fit in, because you think it's expected of you or because it may be the way things have always been done within your family or business for years.

You have started to outline your plan, your goals and your dreams and how you will achieve them. Writing the plan is easy enough however following the plan and taking the required action every day is another matter and it's easy to fall back into your old habits and old ways and fill your brain with fog. You have crafted many of those habits over a life time and they are well known to you and very comfortable.

A key thing to remember is the old saying "Rome wasn't built in a day". Taking back control of your life starts with understanding who you are and what is important to you.

Remind yourself about your core values, we looked at these at the beginning of the book and remember this is about you. You need to learn to take care of yourself and dedicate some time to you and your well-being. It's ok to have a "me" day, switch your phone off and do whatever makes you happy, read a book, leave your pyjamas on and curl up on the sofa and watch a movie.

Learn to say "no". It's easy to be there for everyone, your colleagues, your family, your social clubs and because you are so accommodating, everyone comes to you with their problems. You are so nice, why would you say "no". They will understand if you just say, on this occasion " I am sorry, I can't but happy to help another time". Be clear and break the chain.

Don't put things off. How many people do you know who thought they would wait until they retire to travel, to learn a new skill, take time to go on long walks? How many of those people, ironically, died just after they retired and didn't fulfil their dreams? Live in the present as tomorrow may never come.

Try new things, learn to dance, learn a language, learn to laugh more. Yes, laugh more as too many times we are caught in the seriousness of life and then when things change, you look around and ask yourself why? Don't leave the why's until it's too late.

Be open to what the Universe is showing you. The Universe is always presenting opportunities but too many times we are wrapped up in busyness and can't see the opportunities or we get comfortable within the cozy parameters of chaos that we know so well.

Change doesn't need to be cataclysmic, it's ok to take little steps. Many little steps eventually lead to a big leap. Little mindset shifts daily can lead to a whole new way of thinking.

Training your brain to replace negativity with positivity will eventually become second nature once you spot the signs. No different to a child who realizes not to touch the fire as they will get burned and likewise teaching our brain to change something negative into something positive will become the norm.

Keep on track with your goals. When you have clarity and have the passion to get to your end game, you will not allow yourself to get caught up in things that don't matter and don't serve your purpose. This clear purpose, when broken down into small steps, will also become second nature.

Be aware constantly. When your antenna is tuned in to your future goals and your existing needs, you will be aware of things and people who drain you. Not only do you need to train your brain to park negative thoughts and change them with positive thoughts, you also need to be aware of negative people who will drain the life out of you. These people will drag you down and make you feel hopeless, quite often making themselves feel great.

Don't let other pass their baggage onto you. You don't need unnecessary weight on your life's journey.

Be honest with yourself at all times. We need to stop from time to time and look inwards and take a spot check on what we are doing, who we are mixing with and where we are heading. No point of fooling ourselves we are on our life's path when we know deep down, we are in an environment or with people who don't have our best interests at heart. But that's ok – as long as you see it and take action to change it and let those things and people go and not allow them to create havoc in your life.

Sometimes in life there are things you can't change and it's not your job to change other people. You have enough to do getting yourself on track. Keep your focus.

Just remember to live your life and don't kill your dreams.

TAKE CONTROL OF YOUR LIFE - GET OUT OF THE FOG

1) **How many times have you just gone along with things in order to fit in or for a quiet life? When and how?**

   In relationships:

   _____

   _____

   _____

   _____

   _____

   _____

In your workplace:

_____

_____

_____

_____

_____

_____

_____

_____

_____

_____

_____

_____

By compromising your beliefs and core values, in reflection, how does this make you feel?

_____

_____

_____

_____

_____

_____

_____

_____

_____

_____

_____

2) **On what occasions have you said yes to something or someone when you really wanted to say no?**

_____

_____

_____

_____

_____

_____

_____

_____

_____

_____

_____

3) How can you protect yourself from now on by only agreeing to things that you truly want to do?

_____

_____

_____

_____

_____

_____

_____

_____

_____

_____

_____

4) **What negative thoughts regularly creep into your brain and how can you train your brain to replace those with positive thoughts?**

_____

_____

_____

_____

_____

_____

_____

_____

_____

_____

_____

5) **Who do you have in your life that creates negativity?**

In relationships:

_____

_____

_____

_____

_____

_____

_____

_____

_____

_____

_____

In the workplace:

_____

_____

_____

_____

_____

_____

_____

_____

_____

_____

_____

_____

6) How are you going to eliminate the negativity caused by these individuals and protect yourself?

_____

_____

_____

_____

_____

_____

_____

_____

_____

_____

_____

_____

7)   It is your gift to yourself to retain your clarity and take control of your life... you owe it to yourself. List at least 5 things you will do each day to remind yourself that you are the one who is in the driving seat.

1. _____

_____

_____

2. _____

_____

_____

3. _____

_____

_____

4. _____

_____

5.

CHAPTER 8

SELF DOUBT >
SELF CONFIDENCE >
SELF WORTH

Socrates said ....
"Everyone wants to tell you what to do and what's
good for you.
They don't want you to find your own answers,
they want you to believe theirs"

As children we were taught to behave according to what our parents or guardians thought was acceptable. We were either praised for being good or punished for being bad.

Progressing through our years from childhood, to teens, to adulthood those assessors of our life's actions continued.

Life stage	Assessor
Infants	Parents/Guardians
School	Teachers
College/University	Professors
Work	Managers/Bosses
Relationships	Partners
Parenthood	Children

During those years from being told what to do as a child by your parent or guardian, to coming full cycle as a parent and being conscious of the opinions of your children, we adapted our behavior to what we deemed acceptable to our assessors.

In our childhood we had no fear of expressing our opinions however as we grew up, we lost some of that freedom and adapted our behavior to fit in to social norms. We shifted our focus from self-confident free thinking individuals to social game playing, indecisiveness and prejudging situations before venturing forward with our thoughts and ideas. Would they be acceptable, would they be judged, would they comply with other people's opinions? This cycle eroded our free spirit and limited our self-confidence to voice our opinions based on our inner wisdom.

How can we bring back that spirit and release our inner wisdom without fear of retribution? Firstly, we need to be self-aware.

Self-doubt:

How many of us procrastinate on making decisions or taking steps forward to the extent of inaction? Can I? Should I? What will they say? What if? Your belief system has been created over many years and put you in a place where you doubt everything you do and your ability to change.

Heads and hearts filled with self-limiters we can talk ourselves out of anything that involves change by thinking "it's not possible, I can't do it, I am not good enough, I don't deserve, someone else should do it, I will fail". Really? What's the worst thing that can happen? You may even succeed! Imagine how that is going to feel.

You can put those steps in place to make changes immediately. Why wait? Be confident, nothing is impossible with a little guidance and your desire to move forward.

Self-confidence:

When you are self-confident you will shine like a bright star. You have a belief in yourself and your abilities although your mind state can shift depending on circum-stances you are in at any one time. Often the most self-confident person can take a confidence knock. However, it is their ability to pick themselves back up and get back on track that sets them aside from the self-doubters, or some-one generally lacking self-confidence. Those self-doubt-ers have the knack of beating themselves up and staying in a dark hole without being able to visualize a way out.

When you have self-confidence and belief in your abilities you will display clarity of purpose, be proactive and assertive in your drive to achieve your goals and am-bitions. Self-confident people bring out the best in others around them. They share a light that is infectious and you want to be around them as their energy flows like a river and you want to get in that river and swim with them. Self-confident people feel worthy, not afraid of making decisions, feel self-worth, feel they can achieve and hap-py to ask others for their support. Self-confident people feel and demonstrate gratitude which comes back ten-fold from the Universe and the law of attraction. Be aware who you spend your time with and avoid those who are like vampires sucking the life out of you.

Self-worth:

The dictionary definition of self-worth is "sense of one's own value or worth as a person".

Self-worth is about you and who you are, what you do for yourself and for others. When you are aware of your self-worth, you are aware of your inner voice and how in your quietest, weakest moments it can creep in and be destructive. When you are at one with yourself, you know how to tame that inner voice and keep its nastiness at bay. At its worst, the inner voice throws some negativities about who you are and what you deserve, how you should be in comparison to others either in looks or activities that others partake in. These at their most horrible can lead people to moments of despair, to drugs, to bingeing, to eating disorders or alcohol abuse. The mind is a delicate instrument and your sense of self-worth can be in and out of tune depending on your latest successes or failures.

Keeping your self-worth intact is an on-going part of maintaining your well-being because when you take your eye off your self-worth, that inner critic will be there like a shot.

Pursue activities and a lifestyle that are meaningful to you and in line with your own personal core values that we looked at the beginning of the book.

- Be kind to yourself – if you can't look after yourself, how can you be kind to others.

- Remember that nobody is perfect and we can all make mistakes. Maintaining your high self-worth, means you pick yourself right back up and get back on track.

- Challenge your inner voice when it is being critical and keep your faith in yourself and your abilities.

- Nourish your brain and your body and be aware of what you are consuming

- Don't allow external influences to take you off track and shake your resolve.

- Retain your feeling of worthiness – you deserve the best.

SELF DOUBT >
SELF CONFIDENCE >
SELF WORTH

1) **When have you doubted yourself and your abilities?**

What was the situation? Relationships:

In relationships?

_____

_____

_____

_____

_____

_____

_____

In work?

_____

_____

_____

_____

_____

_____

_____

_____

_____

_____

_____

_____

2) **Of those areas where you had doubt, what was the actual outcome?**

_____

_____

_____

_____

_____

_____

_____

_____

_____

_____

_____

_____

3) **You can control your inner voice – talk back to your inner critic – "yes I can"!**
   What will you say to your inner critic to silence it?

   What is the voice saying? What will you say to silence the voice?

   _____

   _____

   _____

   _____

   _____

   _____

   _____

   _____

   _____

4) **What are you good at? What are your skills?**

_____

_____

_____

_____

_____

_____

_____

_____

_____

_____

_____

_____

5) **What do people like about you?**

_____

_____

_____

_____

_____

_____

_____

_____

_____

_____

_____

_____

6) Remember your dream – what do you want to achieve?

_____

_____

_____

_____

_____

_____

_____

_____

_____

_____

_____

_____

7) Of the skills you listed in number 4 and what people like about you in number 5, how will you use those to help you achieve your dream?

_____

_____

_____

_____

_____

_____

_____

_____

_____

_____

_____

8) **To keep you on track, which friends will you ask to support you?**

_____

_____

_____

_____

_____

_____

_____

_____

_____

_____

_____

_____

CHAPTER 9

YOUR CONSCIOUS MIND -V- YOUR SUB CONSCIOUS MIND

It takes focus, determination and effort to keep you on track to achieve your goals and your dreams. It is said we have little angels sitting on one shoulder and little devils sitting on the other fighting for our attention and battling for supremacy. The angel represents your conscious mind and the devil represents temptation, it's like knowing you shouldn't eat that big chocolate cake and the tempting devil saying, "go on, go on, you know you want to". The reality is, you are the referee in the middle, deciding who will be the winner. If you are not in the conscious moment, knowing what is best for you, the devil on your shoulders will seize the weak moment and win the game and you won't realize until it's too late. Live in the conscious, live in the now, be aware where you are going and what is best for you.

The journey of awareness of our mind's consciousness goes back to Mayan and Incan times. Both Mayan and Incan cultures believed we had multiple levels of consciousness which impacted on our health, spirituality and moral being.

Subsequently many Eastern and Western philosophers, following extensive study, developed their concepts relating to levels of consciousness. One of the most popular theories of consciousness was developed by Psychoanalyst Sigmund Freud. In one of his theories, he defined three levels - unconscious (id), the preconscious (ego) and the conscious (superego). His concept of consciousness related to thoughts above and below the surface often depicted as an image of an iceberg with the small tip above the water (the conscious state); preconscious just below the water and the unconscious deeper and further away from the surface. In simple terms, conscious is the smallest part of the three levels and this is the part of the mind that holds your current thoughts, feelings and your awareness. The preconscious, which is a small to medium part, is your recent memories and stored knowledge. The unconscious part, the largest and most enormous part, relates to things that you have buried in your consciousness – your fears, your irrational wishes, your selfish needs, shameful experiences and things you wish you hadn't done.

The reality is, those things that you have pushed away relating to the past, cannot be changed however you can learn from them. In your conscious state, you can be aware of your present, be aware of how you want to live today and plan your journey to success and happiness.

When you feel negative thoughts creeping in, take a breath, smile and ground yourself firmly in your conscious state of mind. Take a second, look around you and be grateful for everything you have. It would be crazy to think you will never have negative thoughts. We are human beings, things are happening around us all the time and we will never stop that. If you have just broken up from a relationship, lost a job or lost an important game, you are not going to feel on top of the world at that moment. That's ok. It's ok not to be ok all the time. However, it is not ok to stay in the mode as that becomes destructive and can lead to self-sabotage. You have the power to change, you have the power to move outside of your comfort zone and the power to change your thoughts. It's ok to make mistakes but it's not ok to keep making the same mistakes. Learn from them, they are part of your education. Take a risk, take an opportunity to grow and do something new. Ask yourself why you should limit yourself. Ask yourself why you should feel bad about something. Challenge your mind! Ask yourself what else is possible that I have not considered.

It's difficult to be negative when you are consciously being thankful for what you have, when you are enthused about something new and you are pushing ahead.

Live in the conscious, live in the moment and put a little pin in the devil on your shoulder when it pays a visit and ensure the angel wins.

CHAPTER 9

YOUR CONSCIOUS MIND -V-
YOUR SUB CONSCIOUS MIND

1) When have you had an angel and a devil
   sitting on your shoulders battling for
   something? What was the situation?

_____

_____

_____

_____

_____

_____

_____

_____

2) **What did you do?**

_____

_____

_____

_____

_____

_____

_____

_____

_____

_____

_____

3)   What would you do differently?

_____

_____

_____

_____

_____

_____

_____

_____

_____

_____

_____

_____

4) Surround yourself with positivity. List
    5 things that you are going to do every
    day to reinforce your positivity and keep
    negativity at bay.

1._____

_____

2._____

_____

3._____

_____

4._____

_____

5._____

_____

_____

_____

5) **When your subconscious mind wants to hold you back, list 5 things you will do to resist procrastination.**

1._____

_____

2._____

_____

3._____

_____

4._____

_____

5._____

_____

_____

_____

6) Draw your own Angel picture to remind yourself that the Angel must beat the devil:

CHAPTER 10

THIS IS YOUR TIME –
LOVE YOURSELF

How will you feel when you are living your dream? Your life is a constant journey of self-discovery and that self-discovery will continue until you leave this planet. The Universe is constantly offering you opportunities and the more enlightened you become, the more you will see the opportunities in front of you.

It's not selfish for you to love yourself, in fact it is fundamental to your well-being. You cannot take care of someone else if you cannot take care of yourself. Love is all around you when you open your eyes and your heart to receive it. It comes from all areas, from someone smiling at you as you pass them in the street, to someone opening a door for you. The smallest things are gifts of love. You have heard the saying that love makes the world go around and with all these little gestures that happen every day, they are testament to that.

Putting off loving ourselves until we deem ourselves worthy, having lost weight, getting the right job, a partner or whatever you feel will make you complete, is a destructive thing to do. You are who you are today. Tomorrow you will continue to grow in spirit and enlightenment, but nothing is stopping you loving yourself right this moment.

We have forgotten how to love unconditionally in a world where everyone is trying to shape us. You are you. You are beautiful, inside and out. You were born to be your own special person, accept yourself for who you are. Why wouldn't you?

REINFORCE YOUR STRENGTH TO LOVE YOURSELF

1) Make your dream board – from the earlier chapter, what is your dream, what will it look like?
2) Find a photograph that represents your dream and find a large pin board and create your vision. Know where you are going and when you are going to get there. You need to have a clear goal.
3) Every night before you go to bed, take 5 minutes to visualize your dream and how you are going to feel when you are living in that special moment of achievement.
4) When you get up in the morning, remind yourself of who you are and where you are going. Remember it

takes sixty-six days to form a habit, so persevere, it will be worth it.

5) Remember (in Chapter 1) you created a card the size of a credit card, listing your core values – read these every day and remind yourself who you are.

Daily quotes to keep you on track, voice them out loud to the Universe:

1) I am grateful to be alive and thankful to the Universe for giving me my life and presenting me with opportunities
2) I am going to achieve my dream of......(what your dream is)
3) I love where I am and appreciate everything that is around me
4) I will only surround myself with positive people who love me and care for me
5) I release negative thoughts and I will replace any that creep in with positive thoughts
6) I will be the referee between the angel and the devil on my shoulders to ensure the angel wins and I remain focused on my life´s journey
7) I am grateful for love and worthy of the love that is around me
8) I am excited about the day ahead
9) I am going to succeed and achieve great things today

"THANK-YOU UNIVERSE"

I hope you liked the book and it helps you
create the life you desire.

Need help and guidance to align your goals
with your deepest passion?

JOIN US ON ONE OF OUR EXCLUSIVE
POWERFUL RETREATS

This is your time to take a leap forward, come out
of the fog and live the life you deserve.
TAKE ACTION NOW....TREAT YOUR
MIND, BODY & SOUL

Contact: moira@inamentalfog.com for information
regarding our retreats and our training
and coaching workshops.

It´s your time to shine

Thank you
Moira

Printed in Poland
by Amazon Fulfillment
Poland Sp. z o.o., Wrocław